I enjoy writing. Seeing a thought on pap[...]
writing in the third grade. I rhymed the w[...]
that year and it made me feel invincible.[...]
with them at school", I tattooed to lo[...]
combined an[...]

MW01233524

My love for writing grew when moving to Texas in 2011. I was placed in all AP classes due to the curriculum difference from my hometown, New York. I had no idea what that meant but who was I to argue with the counselors? Maybe I was the genius that they assumed.

Before the flowers could bloom that spring I knew that placement was not for me. I would sit with my headphones warming my ears from the first bell until the last bell set me free into the Texas breeze. I made the trade for regular placement in math and science but remained in the advanced literature class. This was the only room where my interest and intellect would race at the same speed as the instructor.

"How y'all doing", I would hear everyday that year from this polite but stern dark-haired teacher. The first paper I turned in I was confident. The kid from New York. "My friends are cool, they sometimes drool, I hang with them at school" died that day. Not only did I receive a failing letter grade for the essay on a book we had just read, but also a jolt that energized a new way of thinking.

She sat down with me and spoke of a new approach to writing. A way to get the same points across but in a smooth, stylistic way. Rather than just listing and following traits of the infamous *hamburger method*, she explained how style is needed in all forms of writing. I began to attack writing essays as if it was music or clothes--familiar things that oozed with style. It all grew to one channel.

I can't recall her name but I am forever grateful. Honor and light to every teacher who cares beyond grades and memorization. We need you like a parent.

With this book my goal is conversation. These pages all hold experiences. Many that are personal and some from energies that have surrounded me. My method of putting these words on display is an act of growth and a highlight on mental health. The ability to seek what's inside of you, come to terms with it, and move forward.

I hope I make it to your coffee table.

Just! Keep! Going!

By Ronald Peabody

SHELVES

Without ups and downs,
What is direction

Create something beautiful
Admire,
Then sit me down

Admire,
Then do me again

Love,
Moments,
Relationships,
Cycle like wind

And I guess that is fine

But let's not pretend blind,
To the shelf hung with nails

Dust or none
What was made is still

Sits pretty,
Even when moving on

YELLOW TAXI RAIN

I was so used to the rain,
Held both my pockets for the warmth

My clothes have dried
But just for how long
Until the taxi gains it's speed
As it approaches our curb
To soaking every word,
I couldn't say to ya'

THOUGHTS LOUDER THAN THE Q TRAIN

Church avenue blues
You don't even have a clue,
What the world is telling you

You've got to love me too,
This block is big enough for two

Hear the Sunday bells on a Saturday

BEDTIME RIDDLER

No one sees the face,
Even on the best day

For not too long,
If ever you show
I plead my case
To the judge in robe

Knocking nails in a cross,
Hanging me for a thought

Keep swinging, baby
Keep talking in cool

When the light hits strong,
I'll say when gone

Identity

It is you,
All along

PARENT

When the breeze coats the spring,
Like a sun through the screens

Like the words spoke to me
"He can't live,
Fair ain't free"

I'm torn between,
Two burning things
Old blue flames,
Lost in heat
Infecting,
Ash on seeds
Reflecting,
You on me

BLACK

In a sauna,
With windows far in each corner

Reaching the latch is harder,
To adapt is maybe smarter

Endurance is the charcoal,
To the flame sparking no fold

Has the saying grown old
Or is my skin cuckold

Unfaithful
Uncertain
Not settled at home

I mustn't crack,
I am made from gold

Chasing,
Chasing,
Falling down

The rewind button's broken
No mechanic in town

No change or a token,
Can win what was seen
The gleam jumps water,
From the eye obscene

Happy,
Happy
Candid trust?

Coins dance in the well

We fall with no push,
To whoever,
Forever

Happy, happy,
Can trust?

Hope my wish makes the cut

To the fall with no push
To whoever,
Forever

I can be
Your dream machine,
With spanking new batteries

A heart that's sold separately
Your newest toy,
I can be

VOODOO

Learning of,
The song to sing

The one with words,
To add links our brink

Would you look at me,
How you look at me?

I'm wrapped around your figuring

Sight,
Flow,
Lingering

Well,
Won't you look at me?

JOHNNY

Johnny hopes ones day it rains,
Remind him life's more than a game

To see yourself is to be afraid

To show your gain,
You change your name

Pay for your mask and keep the change

Love never grows,
It just remains

The pool's too full,
No more technique
Each stroke is broke by unknown feet

Each day you're bored,
Blame goes to weeks
Don't know if Johnny is a need

"Open the door,
You own the keys
Don't leave next time,
I'll dream you'll cheat"

BABY

New born,
Eyes don't see

Surrounding
Touching technology

Packed and played
Game on game
Plug me in
Fast like a tracking train

I'm in a game on game
Packaged the way I came

O'MAN JACOB

Leaves still fall,
When the season doesn't call

Wonder if they go far,
When the old man rakes
From the yard to the grave,
You play in high stakes
Blue jeans,
Featherweight
We hold until we brake

Will the frame get ruptured?
And live without color?
The cries in buffer,
As I forget my comfort

Daddy was a hustler,
I can't hold on to nothin'

Who am I to puncture
The skin that's been covered?

BLEACHED

Just slipping

In between

Silk sheets

I need my rhythm

Hold me please

New York minute

Talk to me

W-H-Y

You're so interesting
So full of yourself but weightless

Today I am here,
Rocking chair and a blanket
Understanding with,
Belief unmeasured
Who says need be,
For the dish to be of pleasure?

Hide and seek lovely one
The love with cost

The ones I love,
Show me what is won

Number one

Gaze swaying to the sky

Show me you are weak,
You are just like I

We could both be free,
Without care for
W-H-Y?

Just! Keep! Going!

COLORS

Objects much closer than they appear

Door is open,
With a handle weight of a bear

Heavy is the one who cannot clear
All at once,
I'm on my way there

Some lessons rough like American spirit,
Too tough,
Lifespan needs more than the digits

Kiss me
You fool

I can change colors too

Blue to red,
Then blue again
Make me your favorite diamond friend

Blue to red,
Then blue again

I can change colors too

NECK BONE

Walks like feathers in air
Kissing the mouth of a cave,
Why you here?

Travel further time,
On the crooked line
Fears are cries
Dressed down in disguise

Choose what you puppet,
Hands held with the darkness

Setting blame to lovers,
Couped in that apartment

Building a pond with stones

Water is rising,
Up to my neck bone

Dangerously close

I push away everything,
That I know

WIMBLEDON

How to break the circle,
Of the direction made by the men
He was born into it,
Some streets down from Wimbledon

Oh, who knows what is coming?
And those who know, do not know when
Hands to salute for the job running,
The blood below pigmented skin

Just to be so much different,
To see the other side
If this isn't a sign,
Walk with me as blind
To the snow fall crystal,
When the kids all forget
The stories of wisdom,
That a parents once said

Now with time comes a riddle,
Must follow the chance
How much more to the mystery,
Until I see you again?

All the knobs with a jiggle,
Needing more than a plan
Police man blows a whistle,
They arrest him again

No call but to mother
Hope she listens again

He remembers that sweat
Sweet, sweet,
Old stench

Just to be so much different,
To see the other side

Just to take it where,
No one has gone

Oh, my Wimbledon

Tell us we're wrong

Just! Keep! Going!

CURTAINS

Knots in the curtains

Won't attach to what you can manage

Experiment for feelings

Means for your separation

In the loveliest way

Sleeping with pleasure

War is just absence

Even the villain is honest,
I cant say I am

Your mind is not infinite

Your heart,
It measures it

What you no longer can be

Stuck in a body,
That breathes

I'm from a block where,
Brothers go to war

I was a youngin',
When they kicked down my door

Pointing their weapon,
My body start to froze

"Don't move a muscle,
Cause I will let it go"

The uniform,
Cemented from toe to head

The cold floor,
As I slid across,
Knees bent

Sitting in comfort,
Sticking to the said

In handcuffs my loves,
Walk out the door broken

LICE

Fear me no more
Look me in my eyes

Season the soil
Cooking a grow
Rain come in shower
Pour 'till I'm full

Wait 'till I'm old
I'll be tall

Kurt like Cobain,
Jackson to Mikes,
Six to sense,
Take me ripe

I am below just stretching
Rooting for a nourishment

WINDROCK FARM

What you hide just owns you

Black streets,
Four wheels

High beams guide our pursuit,
Shines the animals

Air was still,
Enough to hold in all my smoke

Rouge in vogue,
The poser paints just what I fought

Stuck to me like asphalt,
Filling up and blending parts,
That tension made empty

Stars blue colored,
Zoom in for question

The rust from your fetters,
Chains holding conquest

TRUTH

This morning,
I screamed out the truth
Can't wait another summer to prove I know about the moon

I'm scared
I might save someone new
Meeting up with my potential

FROZEN RIVER

Walking on a frozen river

Keys so much lighter

Finding space for both,
Titles hold like chokes

Three color a sky,
Beauty fills my eye

I wonder over you

Will you ever,
Breakthrough?

Just holding on,
To all but your soul
Can't take back the things,
That you up and sold

Fighting in the dark,
With echoes
Hey little drummer boy
You're just poor

Just! Keep! Going!

SURFACE

Footage from our Olympus camera,
A colorless good riddance

In hopes to not deal with it,
We cope to cut deals with it

Just building on sand silly,
Free falling
Above the clouds and blimps,
Frigid sets the higher we get

Rush hour time,
The shift's close to end
"The money's good",
Listening to them

Opinions don't set spun for a web,
Make up the king size bed in your head

Surface to levels you think is land,
Excuses like boys becoming men

Never too up,
Never too dim
When will you grow,
From where you have been?

PEOPLE

What took you so long?

The speeding car,
The leather trim
The engine hurling from within

What took you so long?

To grab the clutch and burn the rubber
Some people love,
Some people fuck

What's all the rush,
Pots full of luck
The rainbow reaches two of us
Savings for more oxygen

Run no more,
Run no more
Want no more,
Want no more

10/04/2017

When is the last time
My words
You heard

My fear

All my confusion

There's something more,
Than this illusion

I know

But to know is to be calm,
As calm as the shadows walk

There is something,
Crawling limp
I feel something,
That I'm in
I feel something,
Puzzled up

I feel something
So I too,
Can see in the dark

DEALER

Day to night
Smokes to wine

A long ride?
No, just another long night
4 AM eyesight
Does a dance I do not mind

Take my drunk advice until we cannot see,
I have talked too much to fall asleep easy

Thoughts on my skin
Proceeds before speech
Like the newspaper man
"You must buy before peeks!"

Give me a minute
Will return our life to thrill

Every thought in rhyme

Leaves me to spill

Mouth filled to kill

Weapons to deal

Just! Keep! Going!

ONE STAR

I found a pool down this one star road

Lightly lit,
Sometimes dull
Sometimes so happy,
Most times alone
Cars all come down,
And u-turn home

But back to the pool,
With ever clear proof
Of soak and swim,
To find who's who

Without a lesson or a guard,
To blow the whistle when too far,

I come out in a shrivel,
Scaring everyone to death

Face wrinkled,
Clothes drenched,
Who I am?
Take a guess

I'll bet my body to see me again

BABYLON

Eat me alive,
Something spoke from the table

Conversation so thick,
Knife won't cut stable

What if this is a battle,
Souls seek to defeat
Older gods talk in babbles,
To the child who is free

Guinness stout and jealousy,
Swallowed cold and cooked
The wisdom that won't reach,
Text to a book

I'm surrounded by plastic,
An animal caught
Swimming through open ocean,
Dirty like scared cops

Fear is emotion,
Treadmill for a thought

Clouding deepest devotion,
Turn my moon to a sun

MEANDERS

Here and now,
If you can take the dive

Trust that all you know will hallow,
What's behind just will show you

All in line is hoax

Let it go,
Let it go

Racing through meanders,
Shaping what we enter
Undressing questions,
Melting for a lesson

Racing through meanders,
The blind child is *yessa'*,
Drawing but cannot picture,
Shaping what we enter

Racing through meanders,
With a home by the river
Life know just to whither
Shaping what we enter

BUNK SKUNK

Too soft
To break,
Too hard
To fix,
Hit me with,
Your best shot

Empty out your clips

Just! Keep! Going!

VIVID

Try me

The label speaks as bold as I wish

You push me,
Now all my bones are vivid

The closer I get,
Is the further I am
I hold but sweats separates our hands

It's all just painting,
Water colors that run
In directions that move,
Where the winds comes from

From the country or town,
And the city in state
The only thing real is what can be fake

So take me as I am,
I'll come in as you are
Nothing will be hard,
No thinking at all

I FALL IN LOVE SO EASY

Lead the way,
Young lady

My fair lady

The diner food,
Like you,
Hot and ready

I'll relax,
I'll smile,
Upon arrive

My name?
Similar to Eddie,
Freddy or James

Maybe even Pau,
At the middle of the road,
Forgetting lips had once told

You could lead the way,
My heart,
My fair lady

FIGURES

People from the town
They start to turn to figures
Complicates the view,
But what about the children?

Bitter, bitter, glitter,
You just look so familiar

Oh,
The bigger picture can afford,
More of interest

Hang it on the wall down the hall,
For reflection

Holding every story for the one
Who pays attention

Lessen what you're bringing,
Space is small on adventure

Signals hitting me,
The exits all in the mirror

FALL

She falls in love
I fall similar
She falls in a line
My heads vertical
Brace for another life
I hope similar
Treat me like a glove
Moving how you want

COMETS

I won't run
I won't play
When I shoot
I'll be straight to you

Setting up
By the sun
I will not
Fumble what
You threw

Cause comets shoot to destroy things
Starting off so bright then rushing me

I am deep in yours eyes

Thrusting

I am deep in your eyes

Thrusting

FIRE TRUCK

It's alright,
It's alright
Magnify my behinds

Someone out of the crowd,
Adore me as a child
Holds his favorite truck

Love like I won't grow up

STANDARD

New comes soon
Rose color paper with text
Breaking stories
Breaking bodies
A scent never goes hiding

Everyday there is option
To pick you up
To read your palm

Then the morning rushes in
Clouds blossom to the sky
The biggest surprise is the one I am sure
That i have not changed in fact at all

But to give notice is to identify
And with know comes the choice
Grab all you can and run
Or trust that one is all enough

The mature takes the front stage,
At last!
The half hour,
Color going from power to flower then background

Our skin separates slowly,
Spinning webs from sex sweat
Sun rises and shines the face once at rest

An array of beauty marks,
Chiseled angles so sharp
Low sitting eyes,
Dare I ask who and why

Only minutes left
Before the sand in the glass stills
We took noise as the preference
To disrupt our sleep

Another day
Another week
Buckle me up to the beat
Of the rhythm from our feet
From the wood floor to sheets

You physically testing me

Remembering
Remembering

RADIO

I'm not sinning,
Close to calling it
I wanna be a winner,
Not a kiddie kid
Who runs with a scissor
Cutting every picture I don't think I fit in
Hearing is staring in bed

I'm jumping forgetting the fare
I'm taking the way I think's fair

Only owning my feet
Thank the lord, I'm able
I kiss defeat
Lipstick leaves its seat
Jumping from her,
Here to me

Even when doing whatever you want plan is needed. That plan means pressure; pressure in the sense of applied not received. You will understand rather than me asking, "do you?". And if not now, then later. Either way I am freeme.

September 2, 2018 at 2:14 PM

We are all farmers
Farming on the worlds farm
Planting
discovering new formulas for growth
Formulas to fasten
Strengthen
Taste better
  Healthier

There are those farmers who dont add shit lol
Nothing but dead plants
Dead ass plants
watered once a year
Watered bucketload full at once
Or will never get the chance to grow at all

But as a farmer
My mission is to learn from those great farmers before me
Along with me
And those who will be
Use everything as knowledge
And put it into what my passion is
And once again
My passion is farming

My crop is fresh
My crop sometimes I put in the shade
My crop the world knows by heart
I

Its ok to be who I am now
Because I will be so much more tomorrow

@earthcanbeheaven

OUT NOW

SOUNDMATH

EP

Angelnumber 8

:-)

Belor
Ralph
Hawa
Lovette
Jayson
Bennie
Latrell
Khepre
Nathifah
Justin & Jason
Tremaine
Kyle
Danny
Bijou
Andreas
Blake
Wyatt & Nathaniel
Cari
Kim S
Cristofo
Paly
Davis & Sky
Eric & Lonnor
Scott & Butch
AJ
El
Akko
Adrian